DATE DUE

Fish
Life Cycles

BY BRAY JACOBSON

 Gareth Stevens
PUBLISHING

CRASHCOURSE

FX: 09-18

Please visit our website, www.garethstevens.com. For a free color catalog of all our high-quality books, call toll free 1-800-542-2595 or fax 1-877-542-2596.

Cataloging-in-Publication Data
Names: Jacobson, Bray.
Title: Fish life cycles / Bray Jacobson.
Description: New York : Gareth Stevens Publishing, 2018. | Series: A look at life cycles | Includes index.
Identifiers: ISBN 9781538210406 (pbk.) | ISBN 9781538210420 (library bound) | ISBN 9781538210413 (6 pack)
Subjects: LCSH: Fishes--Life cycles--Juvenile literature.
Classification: LCC QL617.2 J25 2018 | DDC 597.156--dc23

First Edition

Published in 2018 by
Gareth Stevens Publishing
111 East 14th Street, Suite 349
New York, NY 10003

Copyright © 2018 Gareth Stevens Publishing

Designer: Samantha DeMartin
Editor: Kristen Nelson

Photo credits: Series art Im stocker/Shutterstock.com; cover, p. 1 aaltair/Shutterstock.com; p. 5 (butterfly fish) Natursports/Shutterstock.com; pp. 5 (lionfish, stingray), 7 (main), 25 Rich Carey/Shutterstock.com; p. 5 (catfish) Kangcor/Shutterstock.com; p. 5 (shark) wildestanimal/Shutterstock.com; p. 7 (inset) Zhukova Valentyna/Shutterstock.com; p. 9 Andrea Izzotti/Shutterstock.com; p. 10 (seahorse) Education Images/Universal Images Group/Getty Images; p. 11 SergeUWPhoto/Shutterstock.com; p. 13 Uwe Kils/Wikimedia Commons; p. 15 Wild Horizon/Universal Images Group/Getty Images; p. 17 Ekaterina V. Borisova/Shutterstock.com; p. 19 Pete Niesen/Shutterstock.com; p. 21 Jeff Rotman/Photolibrary/Getty Images; p. 23 nicolasviosin44/Shutterstock.com; p. 27 Greg Amptman/Shutterstock.com; p. 29 Ramon Carretero/Shutterstock.com; p. 30 Lumena/Shutterstock.com.

Printed in the United States of America

CPSIA compliance information: Batch #CW18GS: For further information contact Gareth Stevens, New York, New York at 1-800-542-2595.

Contents

Words in the glossary appear in **bold** type the first time they are used in the text.

Fresh Fish!

Fish live in bodies of water all over the world. They're vertebrates, or animals with a backbone, and almost every kind is **cold-blooded**. Fish breathe through **gills** and are often covered in **scales**.

Make the Grade

There are more than 30,000 species, or kinds, of fish on Earth.

The many kinds of fish have **adapted** how they live to where they live. However, most fish follow the same general life cycle. A life cycle is the series of steps through which a living thing passes in its life.

Make the Grade

Fish live in so many different places, including the deep ocean, rivers, and ponds. Their life cycle has had to change over time to better assure each species' **survival**.

7

Spawning at the Start

The first step of most fishes' life cycle is called spawning. Female fish let their eggs out into the water. Male fish **fertilize** them using cells called milt. Sometimes there may be hundreds of eggs, though not all of them are fertilized.

Make the Grade

Some fish spawn every year. Others only spawn every few years. There are even fish that spawn once and then die!

Some fish lay their eggs in a nest. Nests might be empty snail shells, a bunch of bubbles made by the male fish, or a hole dug by the female fish. Some fish, called mouth brooders, carry their eggs in their mouth!

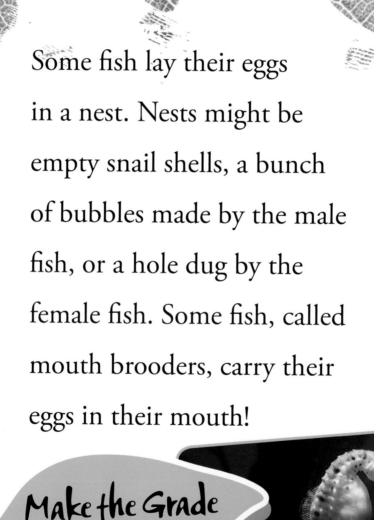

Make the Grade

Male seahorses carry the eggs in a pouch as they're **developing**!

Out of the Egg

Fish larvae hatch, or come out of their egg, after a time. Just-hatched larvae have their own food already on their body called a yolk sac. Once they have taken in the whole yolk sac, the larvae are called fry.

Make the Grade

Young fish are called fry for a few months as they begin to eat on their own and develop more.

fry

yolk sac

13

The changes a fish's body goes through to look like an adult are called metamorphosis (meh-tuh-MOHR-fuh-suhs). Once fry have grown the body parts of an adult fish, such as fins, they're called juveniles. How long this takes depends on what kind of fish it is.

Make the Grade

Many fish don't live beyond the juvenile part of their life cycle. Changes in water temperature, predators, and **habitat** problems can **threaten** their survival.

Adulthood

Juvenile fish continue to develop. Once they're grown enough to **reproduce**, they're called adult fish. For some fish, this is when they're about a year old. But female lake sturgeon (STUHR-juhn) can't reproduce until about age 25!

Make the Grade

The longer a fish lives, the longer it will take for it to become an adult.

The Life Cycle of A Fish

egg

larva

spawning

fry

adult

juvenile

Special
Salmon

Salmon follow the same basic life cycle of most fish, but theirs has a couple of extra steps. When they're ready to spawn, salmon leave the ocean to lay eggs in the freshwater stream or river where they were born!

Make the Grade

Salmon and other fish that **migrate** to freshwater from the ocean are called anadromous (uh-NAH-druh-muhs) fish.

After salmon hatch and become fry, they spend some time in freshwater before they swim toward the ocean. They grow scales and continue to get bigger. Salmon spend between 1 and 8 years in the ocean before they return to their birthplace to spawn themselves!

Make the Grade

After spawning, both male and
female salmon die.

Making a
Manta Ray

Rays are also kinds of fish! The manta ray follows most of the steps of the fish life cycle, with one difference. The female manta ray carries her egg inside her body for about a year. The egg hatches inside its mother!

Make the Grade

Female manta rays only **mate** about once every 2 years.

23

The baby manta ray, or pup, continues to grow inside its mother. Then, the female manta ray gives birth to live young! She commonly has only one or two pups at a time. Manta ray pups can be 20 pounds (9 kg) or more!

Make the Grade

Manta ray mothers have their pup in water near the shore that's not very deep. They leave a pup soon after it's born.

The Life Cycle of a Manta Ray

Adult manta rays mate.

A female manta ray carries an egg for about a year.

The egg hatches inside its mother.

The manta ray pup continues to grow.

The mother manta ray gives birth to live young.

Young manta rays grow into adults.

25

Predator Pups

Sharks can give birth different ways. Some kinds of sharks lay eggs. But most sharks carry eggs that hatch inside the mother shark, much like manta rays. They grow more inside their mother before they're born live.

27

Great white sharks give birth to live young—as many as 12 at a time! Like other sharks, great white pups leave their mother right away. They're already about 5 feet (1.5 m) long, but will grow much more before becoming adults and fearsome predators!

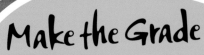

Make the Grade

Most sharks don't live past their
first year because they're eaten
by predators bigger than them,
including other sharks!

29

The Life Cycle of a Great White Shark

Eggs grow inside a mother shark.

The eggs hatch inside the mother, and the pups continue to grow.

Many pups die in the first year; others grow to be adults.

The mother shark gives birth to live young.

Shark pups swim away from their mother.

Glossary

adapt: to change to suit conditions

cold-blooded: having a body temperature that's the same as the temperature of the surroundings

develop: to grow and change

fertilize: to add male cells to a female's eggs to make babies

gill: the body part that ocean animals such as fish use to breathe in water

habitat: the natural place where an animal or plant lives

mate: to come together to make babies

migrate: to move from one area to another for feeding or having babies

reproduce: when an animal creates another creature just like itself

scale: one of the flat plates that cover an animal's body

survival: the act of living through something

threaten: to give signs of being likely to cause harm

For More Information

Books

Amstutz, L. J. *Investigating Animal Life Cycles*. Minneapolis, MN: Lerner Publications, 2016.

Veitch, Catherine. *Fish Babies*. Chicago, IL: Heinemann Library, 2013.

Websites

Fish

kids.nationalgeographic.com/animals/hubs/fish/

Read about many kinds of fish here!

Publisher's note to educators and parents: Our editors have carefully reviewed these websites to ensure that they are suitable for students. Many websites change frequently, however, and we cannot guarantee that a site's future contents will continue to meet our high standards of quality and educational value. Be advised that students should be closely supervised whenever they access the Internet.

Index